Protective Shields Standards:

Addressing the Needs and Requirements of United States Public Safety Officers

Protective Shields Standards: Addressing the Needs and Requirements of United States Public Safety Officers

Contributors

This report was developed by the InterAgency Board for Equipment Standardization and Interoperability (IAB) to describe public safety officer needs and requirements related to protective shields and outline a path forward for standards development. Contributors are identified in table 1 along with their respective organizations and affiliations.

Table 1. Contributors

	Name	Expertise	Organization
1.	Brian Washburn	End user, Law Enforcement/ Bomb Squad	Santa Clara (CA) Sheriff's Office, IAB Standards Coordination SubGroup
2.	Carl Makins	End user, Law Enforcement/ Bomb Squad	Charleston County (SC) Sheriff's Office, IAB Training and Exercise SubGroup
3.	Casandra Robinson	Standards	National Institute of Standards and Technology, IAB Standards Coordination SubGroup
4.	Craig Dickerson	End user, Law Enforcement	Montgomery County (MD) Police Department
5.	Cris Caldwell	End user, Law Enforcement	CA Dept. of Corrections & Rehabilitation, IAB Standards Coordination SubGroup
6.	Daniel Kowalski	End user, Law Enforcement	Cincinnati (OH) Police Dept.
7.	Dario Gonzalez	Fire/Emergency Medical Service/Medical	Fire Dept. of New York, IAB Health, Medical, and Responder Safety SubGroup
8.	David Otterson	Research, Standards	National Law Enforcement and Corrections Technology Center, IAB Standards Coordination SubGroup
9.	Jay DeBold	End user, Corrections	Ohio Dept. of Rehabilitation & Correction
10.	Jeffrey Finn	End user, Law Enforcement	Fairfax County (VA) Police Dept., IAB Standards Coordination SubGroup
11.	Jeffrey Horlick	Standards	National Institute of Standards and Technology
12.	Kenneth Fuller	End user, Law Enforcement	United States Marshal Service
13.	Martin Hutchings	Law Enforcement/ Bomb Squad	Sacramento (CA) Sheriff's Office, IAB Standards Coordination SubGroup
14.	Matthew Duggan	End user, Law Enforcement	Boca Raton (FL) Police Dept., IAB Standards Coordination SubGroup
15.	Michelle Deane	Standards	American National Standards Institute
16.	Nicholas Roberts	End user, Law Enforcement	Unified Police Dept. of Greater Salt Lake (UT)
17.	Richard Brooks	Fire/EMS	Cecil County (MD) Department of Emergency Services, IAB Training and Exercise SubGroup
18.	Rick Lake	Standards	ASTM International
19.	Thomas Nolan	End user, Law Enforcement	Upper Merion (PA) Township Police Dept., IAB Standards Coordination SubGroup
20.	Patricia Knudson	End user, Law Enforcement	Phoenix Police Dept.

The final report was reviewed and approved by the IAB Executive Committee and Standards Coordination SubGroup.

STANDARDS COORDINATION SUBGROUP

Protective Shields Standards: Addressing the Needs and Requirements of United States Public Safety Officers

Table of Contents

Protective Shields Standards: Addressing the Needs and Requirements of United States Public Safety Officers

1. Introduction

The InterAgency Board for Equipment Standardization and Interoperability (IAB) is a collaborative panel of emergency preparedness and response practitioners, federal employees, and subject matter experts representing a wide array of technical expertise. The IAB facilitates the exchange of knowledge and ideas to improve national preparedness and promote interoperability and compatibility among local, state, and federal response communities. One of the missions of the IAB is to advocate for and assist with the development and implementation of performance criteria, standards, test protocols, and technical, operating, and training requirements for all-hazards incident response equipment.

In 2013, the IAB identified a need for one or more new standards to define performance requirements and test methods for protective shields used by United States (U.S.) public safety officers, including tactical and patrol law enforcement, bomb squads, corrections, fire fighters, and emergency medical services (EMS). These officers purchase and carry hand-held ballistic and riot shields to be used in the course of their duties and need to have confidence that these shields will perform as expected, which is the purpose for standards. As an initial step in the development of such standards, the National Institute of Justice (NIJ) requested that the IAB determine the current needs and requirements of public safety practitioners for protective shields and a develop a path forward for the development of standards.

The IAB convened a group of practitioners[1] and subject matter experts to perform this work, and this report will be used as a starting point for development of new standards. End user perspectives and other data were collected via practitioner discussions, a simple survey (See Appendix A) to the IAB membership and other practitioners having experience with shields, and a detailed questionnaire (See Appendix B) to a subset of those who responded to the survey.

Based on practitioner input, subject matter experts in standards and conformity assessment developed requirements, identified relevant existing standards, and outlined a path forward for developing new standards.

2. Data Collection Results and Observations

2.1. Survey Results

51 responses were received from the following categories of practitioners:

- 24 law enforcement.

---

[1] This report reflects the experience and perspectives of the participants and their agencies only and is not based on a nationwide survey of practitioners.

Protective Shields Standards: Addressing the Needs and Requirements of United States Public Safety Officers

- 2 corrections.

- 10 fire fighter.

- 2 military.

- 13 other, such as emergency managers, emergency medical services.

The surveys identified responders who uses shields, the types of shields used, operational scenarios in which shields are used, the expected protection, and other important characteristics of shields. The findings are summarized within this section.

Law enforcement and corrections are currently the largest users of ballistic shields and riot shields. Fire fighters and EMS technicians are beginning to use ballistic shields in high crime neighborhoods where ballistic threats are likely to be encountered.

Ballistic shields are used primarily by law enforcement officers in situations where there is an expected ballistic threat, including high-risk warrant entry, tactical entry, barricaded subject response, officer/victim rescue, active shooter response, and negotiations. The shield is carried until the ballistic threat is eliminated, and then the shield is discarded, due to its weight, until the mission is completed. Ballistic shields are also routinely used during explosive breaching entry to protect officers from secondary fragments, such as door and structure fragments, resulting from the explosion. Ballistic shields are sometimes used in suicide bomber approach and explosive device perimeter activities; however, officers typically do not expect the ballistic shield to protect against fragmentation or blast overpressure from an explosive device.

Ballistic shields are usually made from aramid, polyethylene, or composite materials. If the shield incorporates a view port, the lens is usually made from transparent polycarbonate, acrylic, or similar plastic. Users of ballistic shields expect them to protect against the threats below, which are listed in order of priority:

1) Handgun.

2) Shotgun.

3) Rifle.

4) Blunt impact.

5) Other: Edged weapons, crossbows, hunting bows, chemicals, liquids, thrown missiles, burning materials.

Protective Shields Standards: Addressing the Needs and Requirements of United States Public Safety Officers

Riot shields are usually made from transparent polycarbonate that is resistant to blunt impacts. Riot shields are typically used for riot control in public areas and correctional facilities and for cell extractions within correctional facilities or jails. Other uses of riot shields are for securing the scene following an active shooter incident (e.g., clearing a building, crowd control) and for protection or herding in an incident involving animals.

Other characteristics of importance, besides protection, are described below:

- Coverage: Amount of coverage is by far the most important coverage characteristic, followed by shape of the shield, then curvature of the shield.

- Usability: Ergonomic issues, such as total weight, weight distribution, grips, and supports, are of critical importance to users. Viewport characteristics, including visibility, field of view, and position on shield are the second most important usability aspects. Operational aids, such as self-standing props, built-in lights, and wheels are next in importance. Ease of assembly is somewhat important.

- Maintainability: Ruggedness is of primary importance to the user because the shields are routinely dropped when no longer needed during an incident (i.e., once the threat has been eliminated). The edges of the shield are especially susceptible to damage from dropping, so enhanced ruggedness around the edges is critical. Other maintainability characteristics of importance are below and listed in order of priority:

  1) Ease of cleaning.

  2) Resistance to damage from exposure to temperature extremes.

  3) Resistance to absorption of liquids.

  4) Ability for the user to replace items, including viewports and batteries.

In addition to characteristics, users identified the following information that should be provided by a supplier with each shield:

  1) Identification and description of the type of threat protection provided.

  2) Care and maintenance guidance.

  3) Size dimensions and weight.

  4) Warranty period and what is covered by the warranty.

  5) Safety precautions.

6) Recommended training.

7) Instructions for proper use.

8) Information on interoperability and compatibility with other responder equipment.

2.2. Detailed Questionnaire Results

The detailed questionnaire was completed by the end users contributing to this report (see listing of end users in Table 1) and currently using shields on a regular basis. The questionnaire is included in Appendix B, and the responses for each question are summarized in this section.

Item 1: Types of shields used

Users identified more than a dozen different ballistic shield models that they use, and the manufacturers of all claim compliance with NIJ Standard-0108.01, *Ballistic Resistant Protective Materials*, at specific levels noted below:

o Type IIA (Lower Velocity .357 Magnum; 9 mm).

o Type IIIA (.44 Magnum; Submachine Gun 9 mm).

o Type III (High-Powered Rifle, 7.62 mm (308 Winchester)).

o Type IV (Armor-Piercing Rifle, .30 caliber armor piercing (U.S. military designation APM2)).

Several models of riot shields were identified by users. No claims of conformity with any standard were found in manufacturer information for riot shields.

Item 2: Expected ballistic threat protection

End users expect a level of protection against all handguns and a level of protection against rifle rounds specified in NIJ Standard-0108.01 plus .223/5.56. Although NIJ-Standard-0108.01 does not address shotgun threats, practitioners indicated an expectation that their shields would protect against slugs, rifled slugs, and buckshot.

The basis for expected ballistic protection is most often manufacturer-provided information that may or may not include test data. A small number of agencies perform shields testing on their ballistic ranges prior to purchase, and only one performs additional testing at regular intervals (e.g., every three years) following purchase to verify lifecycle.

Protective Shields Standards: Addressing the Needs and Requirements of United States Public Safety Officers

There are two actions taken after a shield is hit with a ballistic threat. The most common action is to remove the shield from service, after which it may be used for training or demonstrations, kept as evidence, or discarded and replaced. The only other action taken is to return the shield to the manufacturer for inspection and determination of serviceability.

Items 3 and 4: Expected fragmentation protection

Users expect the shield to provide an amount of protection against fragmentation resulting from explosive breaching of a locked door or a bullet hitting a structure (e.g., wall, door, etc.). Most users understand that shields are not intended to protect against fragmentation or blast overpressure from an improvised explosive device, although some minimal fragmentation protection is hoped for.

The action taken after a shield is hit with fragments depends on the level of apparent damage and the type of fragments impacting the shield. The shield is inspected to determine whether to remove it from service or keep it in service. This inspection may be done by agency personnel or the manufacturer and may involve visual examination only or may involve X-raying the shield. If only superficial damage is observed, such as scratching the shield or penetration of the shield's cover/carrier by fragments, the shield will be mended, if possible, and kept in service. If inspection reveals a penetration of the protective materials, the shield will be removed from service and either used for training or demonstrations, kept in evidence, or discarded and replaced.

Item 5: Blunt impact threat protection

Riot shields are expected to protect against blunt impact threats during riot/crowd control, cell extraction, and similar activities. Blunt impact threats experienced by users include the following:

o Hand-delivered blunt objects, such as mop and broom handles, sticks, bats, and improvised weapons.

o Hand-thrown objects, such as rocks, bricks, bottles, books, and improvised spears.

o Large objects, such as locker boxes (>25 lbs.) and furniture.

o Kicking, punching, and body impacts.

Actions taken after a shield is exposed to blunt impacts are similar to those for exposure to fragments.

Items 6 and 7: Failures and typical wear and tear

Protective Shields Standards: Addressing the Needs and Requirements of United States Public Safety Officers

Due to the operational conditions in which they are used, shields regularly experience heavy wear and tear, including being dropped, trampled, thrown, kicked, impacted, nicked, scratched, slammed in doors, and rained on. Shield edges are especially vulnerable to damage, such as fraying and deteriorating. Other reported ballistic shield failures include broken hand/arm grips or straps, cracked or broken viewports, and broken lights or light switches. The single reported riot shield failure is snapping below the hand/arm grips and above where the officer would rest or place a knee against the shield.

Item 8: Exposure to biological and chemical hazards

Shields may be exposed to biological or chemical hazards during use. Blood-borne pathogens from blood, urine, feces, sweat, and toilet water are very likely to get on shields during an incident. Chemical munitions, such as oleoresin capsicum (OC) spray, may be deployed while shields are being used and are likely to get on the shields. In correctional facilities, shields are routinely exposed to chemical cleaners thrown by inmates. It is expected that shields will continue to provide protection following exposure to these hazards.

Item 9: Cleaning of shields

The process for cleaning shields depends on the agency and what the shield is exposed to. For superficial soiling, cleaning may involve wiping with a dry cloth, wiping with a wet cloth, rinsing with water followed by wiping, or washing with soap and water. If a shield has been exposed to blood or other biological materials, a disinfectant, such as a bleach solution, is used. It is expected that shields will continue to provide protection following exposure to cleaning solutions.

Item 10: Typical storage

Storage conditions for shields differ among agencies. The worst case condition identified is storage in vehicles, either in passenger compartments, trunks, or other stowage. The conditions in vehicles can vary greatly depending on the geographic location and weather. In-vehicle temperatures can range from below 0 °F to above 160 °F, with humidity also greatly variable. Such extreme high temperatures have caused warping of shields. There could be exposure to ultraviolet light for shields stored in the passenger compartment; however, most are stored in compartments that do not allow exposure to sunlight. Some agencies store shields indoors with at least marginal climate control, and the shields are either hung on brackets or leaned against a vertical surface. It is expected that shields will continue to provide protection following exposure to temperature extremes and humidity.

Item 11: Procurement

The users were asked about the procurement process for shields, and almost all noted that end users are involved in the process or have final approval of the purchase; however, most stated that manufacturer claims are their primary source of information since no standards or certification programs specifically for shields exist.

Item 12: Expected service life

The expected service life for shields varies depending on the type (e.g., ballistic or riot) and materials, manufacturer, and viewpoint of the user. Responses to the expected service life for ballistic shields included at least five years, until the manufacturer's expiration date, until hit with a ballistic threat, or until inspection is failed. Riot shields are expected to last indefinitely unless damaged during use.

Item 13: Injuries due to shield use

Many users of ballistic shields noted that they know of no injuries due to using a shield, but the most common injuries identified are shoulder, forearm, and wrist injuries due to the weight of the shields. Trips and falls caused by temporarily discarding the shield after the ballistic threat is eliminated are also hazards that have been experienced.

3. Requirements

The end user information documented in Section 2 was evaluated by standards and conformity assessment experts and is expressed in terms of requirements within this section.

3.1. Performance Requirements

3.1.1. Ballistic Protection

Shields claimed to protect against ballistic threats must be resistant to complete penetration and should be tested against a number of handgun, rifle, and shotgun rounds representing those expected in the operating environment. Resistance to backface deformation is desired in areas of the shield intended to be in contact with the human body (e.g., hand grips). It is recommended that the performance levels specified in the most current version of NIJ Standard-0101 be adopted for shields (*Note: NIJ Standard-0101.07 is currently being developed*).

The following items must be considered:

- Near-edge shots are of concern (i.e., shots within one inch of the shield edge).

- Multiple shots are of concern, and it is recommended that any test methods require a multi-shot group (possibly two or three) within a specified diameter pattern that can be randomly moved around during testing to be sure that test cannot be manipulated.

- Discontinuities or points of apparent weakness must be tested. For this reason, it is important that a build sheet and diagram of construction be provided for the shield model.

- Any attachments and attachment points of the shield must be tested and demonstrate that protection is not reduced nor are any secondary projectiles produced.

- Factory-installed mounting points or attachments for additional equipment must not negatively impact ballistic performance.

3.1.2. Fragmentation Protection

Shields claimed to protect against fragmentation must be resistant to complete penetration and should be tested using fragment simulating projectiles representing those encountered during explosive breaching.

3.1.3. Impact Protection

Shields claimed to protect against impact must be resistant to damage from impacts by blunt and sharp objects and should be tested using simulated test threats representing those expected in the operating environment. Testing methods must take into account the distance between shield and test threat, the test threat delivery method (representing hand-delivered or thrown), and impact velocity.

Any viewports or transparent materials intended for viewing must be resistant to cracking, crazing, shattering, or other damage from anticipated threats (per ANSI specification Z87).

3.2. Usability Requirements

3.2.1. Ergonomics

- The total weight and weight distribution of the shield must not negatively impact the user's ability to perform tasks required during tactical operations.

- Grips and supports must allow the user to comfortably hold and position the shield.

3.2.2. Viewports and Viewing Areas

- Any transparent regions of the shield intended for viewing must be resistant to haze, distortion, discoloration, darkening, and other degradation that could negatively impact the user's ability to see through the transparent region.

3.3. Maintainability Requirements

3.3.1. Environmental Resistance

All shields must be able to withstand environmental conditions encountered during use and continue to provide protection. This capability should be assessed by performing the following conditioning:

1) The shield must withstand heat and cold since transport and storage in a vehicle are typical. The shield must be subjected to hot and cold extremes with testing of protective capabilities performed in each condition. Humidity must be included in the conditions.

2) The shield must be exposed to temperature cycling prior to testing to simulate degradation over time.

3) The shield must be exposed to water submersion prior to testing.

4) The shield must be exposed to solar radiation prior to testing.

The shield must demonstrate resistance to dropping by the user, and this may be accomplished by conditioning prior to testing of protective capabilities.

3.4. User Guidance

It is recommended that a guidance document directed toward the end users be developed explaining details that cannot be addressed within equipment standards. Examples of such details are below:

- Coverage - area of coverage, curvature and shape of shields.

- Location and size of viewport.

- Operational aids, such as self-standing props, built-in lights, and wheels.

- Purchasing considerations.

3.5.   Labeling and Documentation

3.5.1. Shield Labeling

The shield must have a permanently fixed label containing the following information:

- Name and legal address of the supplier.

- Address of manufacturing location (city, state/province, country).

- Date of manufacture (i.e., month and year).

- Model number.

- Level of protection.

- Serial number.

- Mark of conformity indicating certification by an accredited certification body.

- Warranty period.

3.5.2. Documentation

The shield must have supplier-provided documentation including at least the following warnings, information, and instructions:

- Types of threats that the shield is designed to protect against.

- List of components and required accessories provided with the shield.

- Availability of replacement parts.

- Pre-use information as follows:

  o Safety considerations.

  o Recommendations and precautions regarding the application of public safety agency markings, labels, adhesives, paints, or other items after purchase.

  o Instructions for assembly and precautions regarding installation of attachments or modifications to the shield.

Protective Shields Standards: Addressing the Needs and Requirements of United States Public Safety Officers

  - o Warranty information, including time period and what the warranty covers (e.g., performance, workmanship and materials).

- Instructions for proper use as intended by the supplier.

- Training recommendations for shields.

- Care and maintenance, as follows:

  - o Cleaning instructions and precautions.

  - o Recommended disinfection methods[2].

  - o Recommended storage conditions and life expectancy under those conditions.

  - o Inspection details.

  - o Repair methods, where applicable.

  - o Recommendations about replacement of the shield.

  - o Retirement and disposal criteria and considerations.

4.   Existing Standards or Activities Having Applicability to Shields

Given the requirements described in Section 3, research was done to identify standards that may be applicable to the assessment of protective shields, and standards appearing to be relevant are listed and described within this section. This is not an exhaustive listing of standards but rather is a basis from which to continue work.

4.1.   American National Standards Institute (ANSI)

4.1.1.   ANSI/ASSE Z87.1-2003, *Occupational and Educational Personal Eye and Face Protection Devices*. 2003. Washington, DC: American National Standards Institute.

This standard sets forth criteria related to the description, general requirements, testing, marking, selection, care, and use of protectors to minimize or prevent injuries, from such hazards as impact, non-ionizing radiation and chemical type injuries in occupational and educational environments including, but not limited to, machinery operations, material welding and cutting, chemical handling, and assembly operations.

---

[2] End users expect that shields will be exposed to biological hazards; however, there is no existing guidance for determining whether disinfection methods are successful. The best option currently is to follow manufacturer guidance for disinfecting shields.

4.2.   ASTM International

4.2.1.   ASTM WK45341, Work item to develop a standard test method for ballistic resistant shields.

This document is currently under development. The standard will provide a standardized test method for evaluating a shield against a single ballistic threat and describe methodology for evaluating the shield strike face and the performance of the common elements found in a shield design (e.g., viewports, grips).

4.2.2.   ASTM Standard D1003-00, 2000, *Standard Test Method for Haze and Luminous Transmittance of Transparent Plastics*, ASTM International, West Conshohocken, PA, 2000, DOI: 10.1520/D1003-00, www.astm.org.

This test method covers the evaluation of specific light-transmitting and wide-angle-light-scattering properties of planar sections of materials such as essentially transparent plastic. A procedure is provided for the measurement of luminous transmittance and haze.

4.2.3.   ASTM Standard D1044-13, *Standard Test Method for Resistance of Transparent Plastic to Surface Abrasion*, ASTM International, West Conshohocken, PA, 2000, DOI: 10.1520/D1044, www.astm.org.

This standard test method describes a procedure for estimating the resistance of transparent plastics to one kind of surface abrasion by measuring the change in optical properties.

4.2.4.   ASTM Standard F2912-11, *Standard Specification for Glazing and Glazing Systems Subject to Airblast Loadings*, ASTM International, West Conshohocken, PA, 2011, DOI: 10.1520/F2912-11, www.astm.org.

This specification covers exterior windows, glazing panels, glazed curtain walls, and other glazed protective systems used in buildings that may be subjected to intentional and accidental explosions. The specification is designed for all glazing, glazing systems, and glazing retrofit systems such as those fabricated from glass, glass-clad plastics, plastic, laminated glass, glass/plastic glazing materials, and organic coated glass.

4.2.5.   ASTM Standard F1642–12, *Standard Test Method for Glazing and Glazing Systems Subject to Airblast Loadings*, ASTM International, West Conshohocken, PA, 2012, DOI: 10.1520/F1642-12, www.astm.org.

This test method sets forth procedures for the evaluation of hazards of glazing or glazing systems against airblast loadings. The data obtained from testing under this method shall be used to determine the glazing or glazing system hazard rating using ASTM Standard F2912. This test method is designed to test and rate all glazing, glazing systems, and glazing retrofit systems including, but not limited to, those fabricated from glass, plastic, glass-clad plastics, laminated glass, glass/plastic glazing materials, and film-backed glass.

4.2.6. ASTM Standard F1233 - 08(2013), Standard Test Method for Security Glazing Materials And Systems, ASTM International, West Conshohocken, PA, 2013, DOI: 10.1520/F1233, www.astm.org.

This test method sets forth procedures whose purpose is limited to the evaluation of the resistance of security glazing materials and systems against the following threats: *Ballistic Impact, Blunt Tool Impacts, Sharp Tool Impacts, Thermal Stress,* and *Chemical Deterioration.*

4.3. British Standards Institution

4.3.1. BS 7971-3:2002 - *Protective clothing and equipment for use in violent situations and in training. Personal defence shields. Requirements and test methods*, British Standards Institution, London, United Kingdom, 2002, www.bsigroup.com.

The standard addresses two levels of protection. Level 1 is the lower level of protection and requires the shield to pass a blunt and pointed impact test after both storage at 20 degrees centigrade and after being subject to flammability pre-treatment. Level 2 is a higher level of protection in that it requires the same tests as Level 1 plus additional requirements. Level 2 requires impact tests when subject to exposure to various chemicals and an edge impact cut test to simulate a machete-type attack. This test involves the shield being placed vertically under a falling carriage fitted with a sharp blade striker. The penetration of the blade into the edge of the shield is measured.

4.4. Canadian Standards Association (CSA)

4.4.1. CAN/CSA Z617-06 (R2011), *Personal Protective Equipment (PPE) for Blunt Trauma.* Canadian Standards Association, Mississauga, Ontario, 2006, www.csagroup.org.

This standard applies to personal protective apparel intended to provide protection to the torso, arms, and legs, including joints, of correctional officers and law enforcement personnel from blows with blunt objects (e.g., rocks, stones, glass bottles, pipes, baseball bats, wooden planks, etc.) during riots, inmate control situations, and in any other situation in which there is a threat of violent attack to the torso, arms, and legs.

4.5. International Organization for Standardization (ISO)

4.5.1. ISO 13468-1:1999, *Plastics--Determination of the Total Luminous Transmittance of Transparent Materials*, International Organization for Standardization, Geneva Switzerland, 1999, www.iso.org.

This standard covers the determination of the total luminous transmittance, in the visible region of the spectrum, of planar transparent and substantially colorless plastics, using a double-beam scanning spectrophotometer.

4.5.2. ISO 14782:1999, *Plastics--Determination of Haze of Transparent Materials*, International Organization for Standardization, Geneva Switzerland, 1999, www.iso.org.

This standard specifies a method for the measurement of haze, an optical property resulting from wide-angle scattering of light, in transparent and substantially colorless plastics.

4.6. North Atlantic Treaty Organization (NATO)

4.6.1. STANAG 2920 (Edition 2), *Ballistic Test Method for Personal Armor Materials and Combat Clothing*, NATO Standardization Agency, Brussels Belgium, 2003.

4.7. Underwriters Laboratory (UL)

4.7.1. UL 752, *Standard for Bullet-resisting Equipment*, Underwriters Laboratory, Northbrook, IL, 2013, www.ul.com.

These requirements cover materials, devices, and fixtures used to form bullet-resisting barriers which protect against robbery, holdup, or armed attack such as those by snipers. This standard can also be used to determine the bullet resistance of building components that do not fit the definition of equipment, such as windows, walls, or barriers made out of bullet resistant materials.

4.8. U.S. Government

4.8.1. MIL-DTL-43511D, *Detail Specification, Face Shields, Flyer's Helmet, Polycarbonate*, U.S. Department of Defense, Washington, DC, 2006.

This specification covers general and performance requirements for curved polycarbonate flyer's helmet visors worn by aircrew personnel.

4.8.2. MIL-STD-662F, *V50 Ballistic Test for Armor*, U.S. Department of Defense, Washington,

DC, 1997.

The purpose of this standard is to provide general guidelines for procedures, equipment, physical conditions, and terminology for determining the ballistic resistance of metallic, nonmetallic and composite armor against small arms projectiles. Test threats include fragment simulating projectiles.

4.9. United Kingdom

4.9.1. UK/SC/5449, *Specification for Ballistic Test Method for Personal Armours and Lightweight Materials*, UK Ministry of Defence, Defence Clothing, Bicester, UK, 1996.

The aim of this specification is to establish guidelines for the conduct of ballistic tests which are designed to measure the level of protection which is provided by armours or the materials which are intended to be used in armours. Test threats may be fragment simulating projectiles.

5.   Path Forward

This document is intended to serve as a starting point for standards development activities addressing end user needs and requirements, and recommended next steps are outlined below:

1) Evaluate existing standards (those listed within Section 4 and others) against the requirements of Section 3 to determine those standards that should be adopted or adapted as part of a suite of protective shields standards.

2) Identify new standards that are needed, including test methods, specifications, guides, or practices.

3) Identify and contact appropriate standards development organizations regarding interest and willingness to lead or participate in the effort.

4) A comprehensive plan for developing a suite of standards should be created, and the plan should identify needed resources, including stakeholder organizations, types of expertise, research, and funding.

6.   Summary

Protective shields are currently in use by many responders who need to have confidence that their shields will perform as expected. While there are many applicable standards that may have relevance to protective shields, standards development work is required to fully meet the needs and requirements of U.S. public safety officers. The IAB has a broad base of shields users and technical experts with relevant experience and knowledge that can assist in development of standards.

**Please contact the InterAgency Board at info@interagencyboard.us with any comments, feedback, and questions. Additional information on the InterAgency Board is available at www.IAB.gov.

STANDARDS COORDINATION SUBGROUP

Protective Shields Standards: Addressing the Needs and Requirements of United States Public Safety Officers

Appendix A. Survey

Instructions: Please read the scope below and indicate your answers to each item in the questionnaire to the best of your personal knowledge and experience. Select "Not applicable" for any item that is beyond your knowledge or experience.

Scope: The type of protective shields being addressed in this questionnaire are person-deployed, portable, 'non-permanently installed' shields. This includes rigid shield (e.g., hand-carried shields, rolling shields, multi-shield interlocking systems) and flexible/soft shields.

Items not being addressed within this questionnaire include ballistic blankets, bomb blankets, or permanently installed structures, such as those for entry ways, judge's benches, etc.

Item 1: Indicate your primary function:

- Law enforcement officer
- Corrections officer
- Military
- Fire fighter
- EMS
- Other: _____
- Not applicable

Item 2: Indicate your years of experience as a responder:

- < 5 years
- 5 to 10 years
- 11 to 15 years
- 16 to 20 years
- 21 to 30 years
- > 30 years

Item 3: Do you currently use shields? Yes/No

> If you indicated "no", are you planning to use shields in the future? Yes/No

STANDARDS COORDINATION SUBGROUP

Protective Shields Standards: Addressing the Needs and Requirements of United States Public Safety Officers

Item 4: Check the appropriate box to indicate scenarios in which you typically use or plan to use a shield and the type of shield for each scenario:

Scenario	Type of Shield In Use for Each Scenario	
	Ballistic	**Riot (Nonballistic)**
High-risk warrant entry		
Hostage rescue		
Negotiation		
Active shooter response		
Explosive breaching entry		
Suicide bomber approach		
Explosive device perimeter activities		
Officer/victim rescue		
Tactical entry		
Cell extraction		
Barricaded subject		
Riot or crowd control		
Other: _____		
Not applicable		

Item 5: Check all threats you expect the shield to protect against. If known, list specific threats for each ballistic threat that you check:

- Handgun - list specifics, if known: _____
- Rifle - list specifics, if known: _____
- Shotgun - list specifics, if known: _____
- Fragmentation
- Blunt impact
- Other: _____
- Not applicable

Item 6: Indicate the coverage characteristics of importance to you:

- Amount of coverage
- Shape of shield
- Curvature of shield

Protective Shields Standards: Addressing the Needs and Requirements of United States Public Safety Officers

- Other: _____
- Not applicable

Item 7: Indicate the usability characteristics of importance to you. Check all that apply:

- Viewport: Field of view
- Viewport: Location/position on shield
- Viewport: Clarity and visibility
- Viewport: Method of attachment
- Ergonomics: Total weight
- Ergonomics: Weight distribution
- Ergonomics: Grips
- Ergonomics: Supports
- Ergonomics: Carry straps
- Ergonomics: Padding
- Operational aids: Self-standing capability (e.g., shield with kick stand)
- Operational aids: Wheels
- Operational aids: Built-in lights
- Ease of Assembly
- Other: _____
- Not applicable

Item 8: Indicate the maintainability characteristics of importance to you. Check all that apply:

- Ruggedness
- Enhanced ruggedness around the edges
- Replacement of viewport by user
- Replacement of batteries by user
- Replacement of other parts by user
- Ease of cleaning
- Resistance to temperature extremes
- Resistance to absorption of liquids
- Other: _____
- Not applicable

STANDARDS COORDINATION SUBGROUP

Protective Shields Standards: Addressing the Needs and Requirements of United States Public Safety Officers

Item 9: Indicate the items that you believe are important for a shield supplier to provide to users. Check all that apply:

- Identification and description of the type of threat protection provided
- Size dimensions and weight
- Instructions for proper use
- Interoperability/compatibility information
- Care and maintenance guidance, such as storage, cleaning and repair
- Safety precautions
- Recommended training
- Warranty period and what is covered by warranty
- Product Labeling
- Other: _____

Item 10. If you'd like to have input into the development of a standard(s) for protective shields, please provide your name and email address in the space below.

_____

_____

STANDARDS COORDINATION SUBGROUP

Protective Shields Standards: Addressing the Needs and Requirements of United States Public Safety Officers

Appendix B. Detailed Questionnaire

This form should be completed by only those who have experience using shields.

Name: _____

Item	Response	
Item 1: Indicate the type of shields (ballistic vs riot) you currently use, including the manufacturer and model for each type. *If you have a spec sheet for each type, please provide it with this information.*	Ballistic:	
	Riot:	
Item 2: For ballistic shields, indicate the ballistic threats you expect the shield to protect against.	Handgun:	
	Rifle:	
	Shotgun:	
Item 2a: How do you know which ballistic threats your shield protects against (for example, talking with other officers, manufacturer-provided information, training)?		
Item 2b: If your shield is hit with a ballistic threat, what do you do with the shield (for example, keep it in service, repair it and keep using, discard it)?		
Item 3: If you expect protection against fragmentation, specify the source of the fragmentation, and describe a scenario in which you typically use the shield to protect against fragmentation.		
Item 3a: If your shield is hit with fragments, what do you do with the shield (for example, keep it in service, repair it and keep using, discard it)?		
Item 4: Do you expect your shield to protect against fragmentation and blast overpressure from an improvised explosive device?		
Item 5: Describe typical blunt impact threats you have faced during riot, crowd control, or cell extraction events.		
Item 5a: If your shield receives blunt impacts, what do you do		

Protective Shields Standards: Addressing the Needs and Requirements of United States Public Safety Officers

Item	Response
with the shield (for example, keep it in service, repair it and keep using, discard it)?	
Item 6: Describe any failure of a shield that you have experienced (for example, did not stop threat that you expected it to, handle broke, viewport cracked). If you are aware of the failure cause, please also indicate that.	
Item 7: Describe the typical wear and tear your shields undergo during use (for example, dropping, throwing, getting wet).	
Item 8: To your knowledge, has your shield ever been exposed to chemical threats or blood? Describe the scenario in which the exposure(s) occurred.	
Item 9: Do you clean your shields? If so, please indicate what you are trying to remove and what you use to clean them.	
Item 10: Describe the typical storage location (for example, vehicle trunk, in passenger compartment of vehicle) and conditions (for example, temperature, humidity) for your shields.	
Item 11: Describe how your shields are procured for you? Who makes the decision on which shield to purchase?	
Item 12: How long does your agency expect a shield to remain in service and to perform properly?	
Item 13: Has anyone in your agency been injured using a shield or had any ergonomic issues with shields (for example, hand pain from grips, shoulder pain from weight)? If so, please describe.